GOLF TIPS

A STEP-BY-STEP GUIDE TO A BETTER GAME

NICK LUMB

CHARTWELL
BOOKS, INC.

A QUINTET BOOK

ISBN: 0–7858–0541–9

This book was designed and produced by
Quintet Publishing Limited

Art Director: Peter Bridgewater
Designer: Linda Moore
Editors: Peter Arnold, Shaun Barrington
Photographer: Ian Howes
Illustrator: Rob Schone
Jacket Design: Nik Morley

Typeset in Great Britain by
Central Southern Typesetters, Eastbourne

Produced in Australia by Griffin Colour

Published by Chartwell Books
A Division of Book Sales, Inc.
P.O. Box 7100
Edison, New Jersey 08818-7100

Contents

INTRODUCTION

Golf is one of the world's fastest growing sports. Television, with its knowledgeable commentators and probing cameras, has brought international championships into the home. The tournament players themselves are marvellous ambassadors for the sport; they behave impeccably and bring excitement to every event. By its very nature, golf is a game which breeds good manners and courtesy.

This is one sport which the whole family can play together. It is a game that you can play on your own, or as a member of a group. Beginners everywhere are queuing up to learn the skills needed to take up the challenge of the golf course. The working week is getting shorter: which means more players. The retirement age is getting lower: which means more players. People are now more than ever aware of the need for exercise: which means more players. Everywhere, people are taking up this fabulous game.

The system of handicapping in golf enables players of varying abilities to compete on level terms: one of golf's particular advantages. Another asset is the great variety of courses across the world, each posing different problems to the golfer; but even if you were to stick to your local course for a lifetime, no two rounds would be identical. The shot permutations needed to master 18 holes are never quite the same twice; and the variety of skills, the ingenuity and judgement employed each time you take up the challenge, can be endlessly honed and improved.

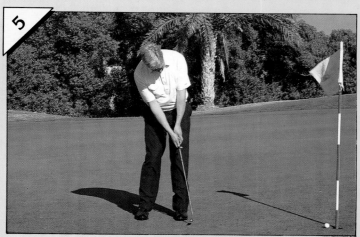

● PUTTING ●

Putting is a pressure shot in golf. It can be the most exciting. In the televised international golf tournaments which make heroes for the more modest golfer to emulate, it is the greens which are the arenas of drama, and the shot which excites both the armchair spectators and the crowd on the course, is the putt which drops.

When you are facing any putt, short or long, do not trust to luck. Watch the care the top players take with even the simpler looking putts. See how they go through the routine of seeking the target line, taking aim, assuming stance – and how they achieve steadiness. You too can become a master of the green.

To putt well, it will help if you understand a little about the construction of a green. Flat greens are optical illusions. Golf course architects cannot build them. The necessary drainage requires greens to have a high and low point. So there must be a slope, which in golf is called a borrow. Often you have to aim off-line to compensate for the slope or borrow. When on the green, look for these high and low spots which will affect your putt. Because of the way greens are cut, the amount of slope on a green can be disguised.

Your putter can be a useful plumb line in assessing the borrow and in finding the target line. Stand behind the ball, lining it up with the hole. Hold the putter out in front of you, thumb and first finger on the grip, shaft pointing vertically downwards and blade pointing out towards the hole for balance. From behind the ball, with one eye closed, line up the straight side of the shaft with the side of the ball and the hole in your vision. You are using the hanging shaft as a plumb line. It will give you an idea of the borrow between the ball and the hole, and how much you need to allow in your putt for the ball to swing in towards the hole.

From anywhere on the putting green – and greens come in a wide range of sizes – your hope is to hole out with one putt. But to take the pressure off the long putts, modify your objective a little. Try to roll the ball close to the hole. Your primary objective is to lay your putt dead, just a tap away from the hole. Your putting standard will improve if you weigh up the length of the grass on the green. If it has been cut that day, the pace will be faster. The way the nap lies will affect speed and borrow.

● FOUR-FOOT PUTT ●

1 When lining-up a putt to help you judge the distance, stand behind the ball and imagine rolling the ball towards the hole. This will help to get the strength right when making the putt.

2 You must take great care in lining up the face of the putter with the hole.

3 Make sure your eyes are over the ball when assuming the address position.

4 A smooth putting stroke must be in your mind when you take the clubhead back.

5 Keep your wrists firm as your putter head goes through to roll the ball towards the hole.

RIGHT AND BELOW RIGHT
To find the amount of
borrow on the green, use
your putter as a plumb
line. The putter should
be gripped between the
thumb and forefinger
and allowed to hang
vertically. The side of the
shaft can be used to find
your line.

OPPOSITE The most
common alternative
putting grip, known as
the reverse-overlap.

Every shot calls for concentration and smooth movement. Remember that each hole on the course is precisely 4¼ inches (107.95 mm) in diameter. Putting is no pushover. It breeds in some players unbelievable reliance upon a particular design or weight of putter and leads to extraordinary idiosyncracies in style, stance and grip. But you should try to putt accurately with the orthodox methods, although your grip may change slightly as you progress.

One rule in putting is never to let the clubhead pass your hands. This common fault arises when you try to anticipate the strike, causing the wrists to flick or break just before the ball is struck. To stop this happening, many players use an alternative grip known as the 'reverse overlap'. With this method the left hand is on the putter grip, with the thumb going straight down the grip. When the right hand is placed in position, the forefinger of the left hand covers the two smallest fingers of the right. The thumb of the right hand also points straight down the shaft. The overlapping forefinger helps keep the arm, wrist, hand and finger all in one line, firming up the wrist. It also keeps the two hands close together, making them work as one unit.

The putt is the only stroke in which you should move away from the orthodox grip. Another, used to great effect by the German champion, Bernard Langer, is the 'cackhanded' grip. For this you place the left hand in a line below the right. This keeps the arms, wrist and hands moving as one unit. It is in some ways a left-handed golfer's grip, used by a right-hander.

Some players favour their trusted putter for short shots from off the green in preference to chipping. This shot has been dubbed the 'Texas Wedge'.

Putting's golden rules are that your eyes must be over the ball and your head must be still throughout the putting stroke. Your whole body should resemble a statue, except for a smooth movement from your arms and shoulders.

ABOVE The golden rules of putting are that your eyes must be over the ball at the address position and that your head must be kept still throughout the stroke.

● PITCHING AND CHIPPING ●

Around the green you will be faced with a variety of shots which demand either short, high flights to leap hazards, or low flighted runs to the hole. The first shot is a pitch, the second a chip. Where you cannot use a putter, a chip is safer than a pitch. As a famous player once said: 'With all greenside shots, always try to make the ball land as near as possible to you.' The point is that, as a general rule, it is easier to judge run than flight; although the speed of the greens is an important factor in deciding which route to take to the hole.

The pitch and chip shots are the foundations of an accurate short game. The loft of the club does the work for both. The pitch will be played with the more lofted club, the chip played with the straighter face.

ABOVE To see the result of your putt, *turn* your head to follow the ball's path to the hole. Do not lift your head to watch the ball.

● THE PITCH ●

A typical pitch shot is the one needed to clear a bunker which guards a green. Stand behind the ball and visualize just where you wish the ball to land, and its flight. Face the hole and swing your arm backwards and forwards, giving you the feel of the shot. Imagine for a moment that you were going to throw the ball. The follow-through would be longer than the backswing. This is also true of your pitch shot. Remembering this will help ensure that you don't stop on the shot: think of it as one-third back and two-thirds through.

In the early stages, it is advisable to play to the widest part of the green for safety. This will make for an easier shot. One thing you do not wish to do is to take your next shot from deep in the bunker. Even tournament professionals do not always aim for the pin, but play 'percentage shots', those which offer the greater percentage chance of success in the end.

Now you have the flight in your mind, select your club and study the lie. You may be tempted to loft the ball with the sand wedge, because that has the greatest loft of all the clubs in the bag. The danger is that if the ball is not cushioned by the grass, the heavy flange of the sand wedge will work against you. The ideal club for a pitch must therefore be the pitching wedge.

For the high pitch shot, assume a stance that positions the ball nearer to the left, or front, foot, forward of the centre line between your feet. Your feet should be fairly close together, the outsides of your feet no wider than your shoulders. Your weight will be slightly more on your left side, with your knees relaxed. This cuts down the transference of weight when you swing the club and helps to keep the body still. This in turn helps you to hit down and through the ball.

With this shot, a slight amount of wrist break is necessary to steepen the clubhead on the downswing, and give a little extra clubhead speed into the ball. When striking the ball, the blade of the club, coming down under the ball, will lift it up and over the bunker to the green. Remember to follow through to ensure you don't 'quit' through the ball. Let the loft of the club do the work. Do not try to scoop. If you do, you are likely to find yourself in the bunker.

The length of your follow-through will be determined by the distance you wish the ball to pitch on the green — and remember you are not relying on much run.

LEFT To pitch a shot, use a lofted club to help give more lift to the ball.

BELOW LEFT To chip a shot, use a straighter faced club. The ball will stay closer to the ground and will have more run.

⬤ THE PITCH SHOT ⬤

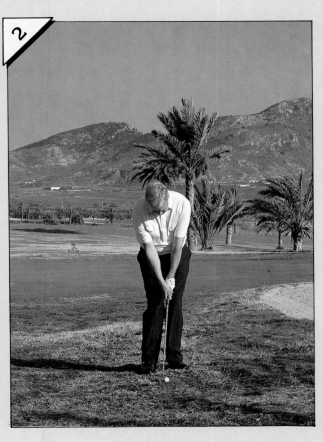

1 A pitch shot is often necessary to clear a bunker. Stand behind the ball and visualise the flight you would like the ball to take.

2 The ball must be closer to the left foot than the right. Keep your feet fairly close together.

⬤ SHOT SAVER ⬤

If you decide to putt from off the green imagine the hole not as a drainpipe but as big as a manhole cover. It would be a huge stroke of luck to hole from such a distance. But by using your imagination like this you could be encouraged to put the ball close enough to hole out next time.

If you take a mid-iron for chipping, the ball does not need to be struck so forcefully because of the lesser loft of the club.

Imagine the shot, face the hole and swing the arm – one third back and two-thirds through. You must not fluff this shot by hitting the ground before the ball. So whereas the width of your stance should be the same as for the pitch, inside a shoulder-width, the ball should be positioned opposite the middle of the space between your feet. Your hands should be opposite your left thigh, with your weight over your left foot. The weight stays there throughout the shot and the only movement is from the arms and shoulders. Your head stays still over the ball.

Because there is no wrist break needed for this shot, the position of your hands assumes even more importance. As you play through the shot, keep the same angle of hands to clubhead; do not let the clubhead fly through because of floppy wrists. There is no place for wrist flicks in golf.

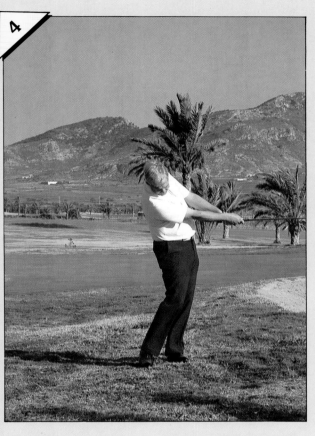

3 A slight amount of wrist break is necessary in the back-swing, to steepen the arc on the down-swing.

4 The length of the follow-through is determined by how far ahead you wish the ball to pitch onto the green. Let the loft of the club do the work. Do not try to scoop the ball.

● THE CHIP ●

The chip gives run to the ball and is used for equally short approaches to the green as the pitch, being preferred where there are no trouble spots to fly over. It is played with a straighter-faced club, like a mid-iron.

Before considering your chip, ask yourself if your putter, used as a 'Texas Wedge', might be more successful. If you were, say, 12 feet (4 m) off the green with 45 feet (14 m) of green to the hole and, using the putter, swept the ball towards the hole so that it stopped 6 feet (2 m) from it, you might feel disappointed. But if you got to the same spot by chipping, you could feel pleased. Your expectations are greater with a putter.

● SHORT IRON PLAY ●

The short iron is played for accuracy and not length. With the 7-iron, 8-iron and 9-iron the ball should be struck from just forward of the middle of your feet, with your hands opposite the left thigh covering your view of the left shoelace. Your body weight should be evenly distributed and your knees slightly flexed. Your feet should be slightly closer together than a shoulder-width. Take a three-quarter backswing. Because of the position of the ball, the clubhead will strike down slightly into the ground, taking a shallow divot, as the hands complete the arc through the ball to the top of the follow-through.

You will find greater consistency if you take a stronger club than you think you need. Do not force your shot. You will be more consistent with

LEFT The ball position for the seven-, eight- and nine-irons should be opposite the middle of your feet with the hands in line with the left thigh.

BELOW LEFT The short-irons are used for accuracy. The length of the backswing is not as important as with the longer shots. Make sure that your backswing is compact. The most important objective is to ensure that your clubhead is on-line.

a stronger club and a shorter, but firmer swing. Let the clubhead do the work, and fight the temptation to scoop the ball.

The shorter irons give height to the flight of the ball, due to the shape of the club and the steeper arc and plane from which the ball is struck. These impart back spin to the ball; when it pitches on the green, very little run will occur.

● MID IRON PLAY ●

The 5-iron and 6-iron have shafts which are a little longer than the short distance irons and are therefore slightly more difficult to use.

To use them, your feet should be a little wider than for the short irons. Strike the ball from opposite a point between your left heel and the middle of your feet. When you stand behind the ball looking down towards the target and seeking the target line, imagine a corridor the width of the green you are playing towards. Try to flight the ball down that corridor. The length is not as important at this stage of the game as accuracy. The ball can always run on. The backswing need be only three-quarters of the full swing. When coming down and through the ball, take very little divot.

LEFT For the mid-iron shot, the stance should be a little wider than for the short-irons. The ball should be between the left heel and the middle of the feet.

ABOVE When playing a mid-iron, keep the swing under control and do not over-swing. The club-face should be square to the plane and the shaft of the club pointing on-line to the target.

● THE FAIRWAY WOOD ●

1 Stand behind the ball to picture the shot.

2 The ball should be towards the left heel as you take up your stance.

3 Push the club back, keeping the arc wide.

● LONG IRON PLAY ●

The shafts of the 3-iron and 4-iron are even longer than those of the mid irons and the concept of swing plane discussed in the previous chapter comes into play. The lie angle of these irons is a little flatter than that of the others, and you will need to stand slightly farther away from the ball. This will flatten your plane and help you to sweep the ball forwards. Beginners should not be too ambitious in trying to carry this shot all the way to the green from the fairway. Look for the corridor towards the green as for the mid-irons.

The feet should be wider apart with these irons than with the others, and the ball position should be further forward, towards the left heel than when using the mid irons. You should not take a divot, and the positioning of the ball towards the left foot will help. Swing and sweep it away off the turf down the 'corridor of confidence' you have set for yourself.

Be careful not to snatch this shot. Build confidence in your backswing to let your body turn and take your body weight through the shot, as it follows your hands.

4 At the top of the backswing, the shoulders should be turned through 90° and the club on-line with the target.

5 Strike through the ball with the correct weight transference. A good finish is essential.

PROVISIONAL BALL (RULE 27–2)

If one of your long iron shots were to go astray and there was a possibility of the ball being lost or out of bounds, it would be tedious to trudge down the course looking for it, only to have to return to the original lie to play a second ball. The rules allow you to play a provisional ball from as close as possible to the original position *before* you go forward to search. When you reach the area where the first ball came to rest, if you find it, then no penalty is incurred and the provisional ball doesn't count. If the first ball is lost, then carry on with the second, losing a stroke as normal.

RIGHT Note the differences between the driver and the fairway wood; the latter has a shorter shaft, a lighter clubhead, and greater loft. The shallowness of the head means its centre of gravity is below the ball, which assists in lifting the ball into the air.

LEFT The straighter face of the driver clubhead makes the shot more difficult to control than the shallower and more lofted face of the three wood.

RIGHT The height of the tee-peg plays a very important part in driving. The ball should be positioned opposite the left heel, with half the ball above the centre of the face and the other half below. The ball is swept away as the club starts its upward climb from the bottom of the arc towards the top of the follow-through.

● DRIVING ●

The drive, taken from the tee, is the most power-ful shot in golf, and can be the biggest trouble finder. It is usually played with the No. 1 wood, but if confidence in your swing is lacking there is no disgrace in taking a 3-wood. Although you are setting up your stance and swing to get the maximum distance with the ball, your main ob-jective is to find the fairway with the shot. The penalty of missing the fairway and finishing up in the rough – in Indian country – or out of bounds, can be disappointingly harsh. So don't gamble with the driver. Play the percentage shot from the tee: try to place your ball down the fairway in a spot where your lie for the next shot is clean, even if you are sacrificing some distance.

The height of the tee peg for the drive is important. Whichever wood you take to drive, you will find the height of the tee peg must rule the position of the ball as you set up your shot. You know that the golf swing is a circle and that the middle of the feet is the bottom of the arc. Therefore the higher you peg up, the further for-ward the ball should be positioned from the centre of your feet. If you tee up the ball on a high peg in the centre of the feet, the driver would sweep under the ball, making it fly off the top of the clubhead.

To use the driver your feet should be at their widest in the stance, the insides of your feet being as wide as your shoulders. As the numbers of the woods increase, so the stance on the tee narrows slightly.

The ideal spot to position the ball for the drive is to tee it up just inside the left foot. This will mean your head is slightly behind the ball. Half the ball should be above the club-face as it sits square on the ground behind it. As you swing into the ball this position allows your body weight to come through, achieving maximum power through your hands, arms and turning shoulders. The ball should then be smack in the middle of the club-face. Keep your head still. Do not let it drift in front of the ball, or that circle swing will loop you into trouble.

Once you have decided to take your driver, you should be totally committed to that shot. Take care to take a full body-turn away from the ball so that you may come back into the ball with a confident, smooth swing and the power to send it out on its way towards the target. And so watch that head. Keep it behind the ball.

LEFT The driver should be positioned just inside the left foot. The feet are a shoulder-width apart.

BELOW The ball is opposite the inside of the left foot and the clubhead is square to the target line.

● THE DRIVE ●

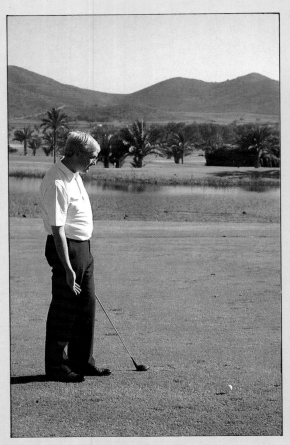

1 The correct alignment of head, feet, club-face and hands during the drive: look for the target line.

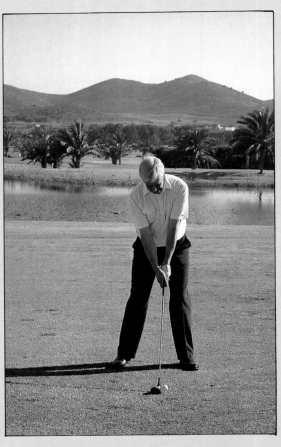

2 The address: note that the hands should be just opposite the ball. CENTRE **3** You will find that the tee itself is a confidence booster. You do not have to worry about the lie of the ball or about your clubhead digging into the ground.

● TEMPO ●

For a full-blooded shot like the drive, the tempo of the shot is important. For the backswing you should take the clubhead back slowly, brushing the ground, until it naturally lifts. The arc builds up and the wrists break at waist-height. Then you make the downward sweep into, and through, the ball.

No high-tech meter can measure and pro-gramme your individual tempo. Mature club golfers carry their own built-in ideas to regulate the tempo of their swing in the full shots. Until practice boosts your confidence a mental trick or two might be useful. Some players seeking self confidence softly hum the opening bars of the main musical theme of the Blue Danube waltz to themselves as they form the swing arc and follow through. It seems to have the right tempo. If it works for you: keep humming. A good drive, after all, is music to your ears.

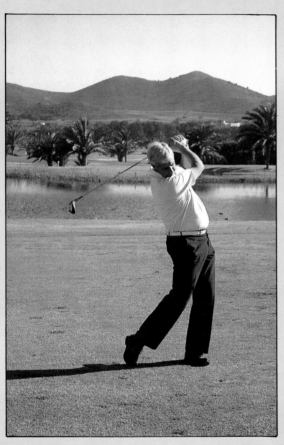

4 Your left side becomes firm while your right leg and right side bend as you come up onto the toes of your right foot.

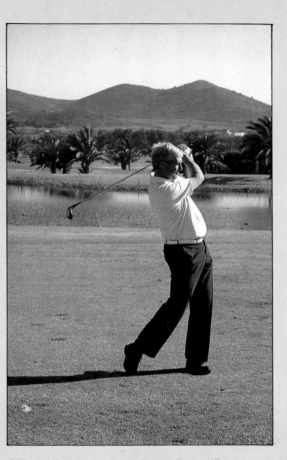

5 The club comes to rest almost diagonally across your shoulders.

● SHOT SAVER ●

A tip I learned years ago came from a veteran Scottish professional golfer, who was asked how to improve the tempo of those big hits off the tee. His dour reply was 'Alexander Cadogan'. I've forgotten who that professional was, but I pass on his tip. Just think of that name as you take the clubhead back slowly ... 'Alexander' ... and down the clubhead swoops through the circle of the arc and out again ... 'Cadogan' ..., the ball being struck on the middle syllable. The rhythm of the syllables is so similar to the different pace of the backswing and follow-through.

Golf shots fly off-line for many reasons. The fault may be in your own hands, your stance, your head position, swing, aim or balance. To identify typical faults you must first understand the concepts of target line and swing line. The target line runs from the ball to the target. That is the line which you take when lining up your shot. The swing line is the actual line taken by the clubhead as it goes from the backswing down into the ball and through to your finish.

If the clubhead goes back and then through on the same line, then it is in plane. If, however, from the top of the backswing you are in an upright position and at the finish of the shot you are in a flat position then you will have swung out of plane, on an out-to-in swing line. The opposite occurs when your hands at the top of the backswing are in a flat position and at the finish of the follow-through have moved into an upright position — then you have swung from in-to-out.

● CAUSES OF BAD SHOTS ●

The causes of bad shots are easiest explained in terms of table tennis. In this game slices and spins are exaggerated and intentional, and the effects easier to see than in golf.

● THE SLICE ●

The slice is a shot where the ball sets off to the left of the target line (still in terms of right-handed players) and swerves in the air to finish right off the target line. The ball has the same flight as the back-spin shot in table tennis. To play this shot the table tennis bat is held open to the target line and the swing line is from out-to-in and the bat cuts across the target line under the ball. The ball swerves from left to right.

● THE SWING PATH ●

The golfing terms for the direction of shot.

● THE SLICE ●

1 This is the same as the back-spin shot in table-tennis. The feet are open, aiming left of the target line, with the bat also lying open.

2 The hands are in an open position at the top of the backswing.

3 To reach the top of the follow-through, the table-tennis bat cuts across the target line, putting back-spin on the ball.

● THE PULL ●

The pull shot goes straight to the left of your intended target line without any swerve. In table-tennis the bat takes an out-to-in swing, coming across the target line, but with the face of the bat square to the actual swing line. The ball would miss the table on the left.

● THE PUSH ●

The push shot sends the golf ball straight to the right of the target line. Its equivalent table tennis shot also flies straight and misses the table on the right. It is effected by an in-to-out swing path with the bat face square to the swing line.

● THE HOOK ●

The flight of a hooked ball starts to the right of the target line and swings in the air to finish left of the target line. In table tennis, its nearest equivalent is the smash, which has an in-to-out swing with the bat face closed to the target line, putting top spin on the ball.

1 The hook is closest to the table-tennis smash. The feet are closed to the target line (pointing to the right).

● THE HOOK ●

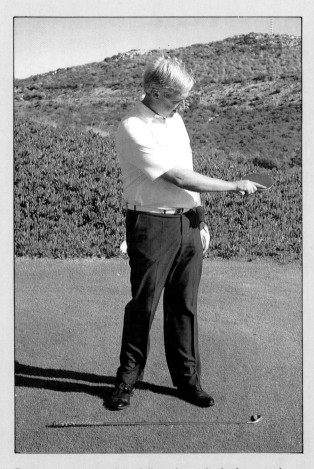

2 At the top of the backswing, the bat is on the inside of the target line.

3 To reach the top of the follow-through, the bat travels from the inside, at the top of the backswing, to the outside at the top of the follow-through. The table tennis bat turns over, closing the face as it strikes the ball, putting top-spin or over-spin on the ball. The flight of the ball is from right to left.

● COMMON FAULTS ●

You must analyze your own game to find any faults with your aim, grip, stance, the position of the ball or your swing to discover the cause of any of your own wayward shots. Listed below are some ideas to help diagnose the possible cause of the trouble.

You might *slice* shots because:

● In your aim the club blade is open to the target.

● Your grip is too weak.

● Your feet or body are lined up left of the target in the stance.

● In your swing, you open the club-face at the start of the backswing.

● Your wrists cup at the top of the backswing, which also causes an open face.

● You are starting the downswing with the right shoulder coming out towards the ball, causing an out-to-in swing.

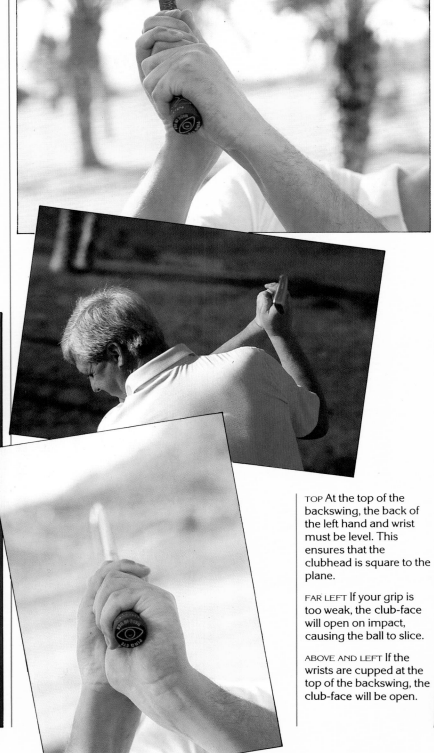

TOP At the top of the backswing, the back of the left hand and wrist must be level. This ensures that the clubhead is square to the plane.

FAR LEFT If your grip is too weak, the club-face will open on impact, causing the ball to slice.

ABOVE AND LEFT If the wrists are cupped at the top of the backswing, the club-face will be open.

You might **pull** shots because:

● In your aim, the club-face is pointing left of the target.

● In your stance and position in relation to the ball, your body alignment is forcing you to the left and the ball is too far forward.

● In the swing you are not transferring your weight properly in the follow-through, but continuing to support your body weight on your right foot.

You might **push** shots because:

● In your aim, the club-face is pointing right of the target.

● In your stance and ball position, the body alignment is forcing you to the right, with the ball too far back from the centre line between your feet.

● In your swing, your body weight is being transferred too early onto your left leg.

You might **hook** shots because:

● In your aim, the blade of the club is closed to the target.

● Your grip is too strong.

● In the stance and ball position your feet and body are facing to the right of the target.

● In your swing you are closing the club-face at the start of the backswing.

● Your wrists are bowed at the top of the backswing, which closes the club-face

TOP If you pull your shots consistently to the left, it could be that your clubhead is pointing to the left of the target at the address position.

CENTRE LEFT Make sure that your wrists are not bowed at the top of the backswing, which will tend to make you hook.

CENTRE If you push your shots consistently to the right, your club-face may be pointing to the right of the target.

FAR LEFT Make sure that your grip is not too strong: this will also make you hook the ball.

LEFT If you close the club-face at the start of the swing, you will hook.

● AWKWARD LIES ●

You will be straying soon enough off the straight and narrow fairways of golf. Do not be too disheartened to find yourself with awkward lies. You may have graduated from pitch and putt courses on which the crisp shots and the soaring golf ball gave you an enhanced view of your ability. You may have come from the driving ranges where you found life and power in your hands, which must now be applied in a wholly different situation. Some of the world's top golf courses are designed in undulating countryside which the course architect wished to preserve, as a challenge to your skills and a pleasant sight to your eyes. He aimed to bring out the best in you. It is up to you now to bring out the best aim for him.

When in an awkward lie, do not be too bold, and watch where you position your weight. These cautions should come into your mind when you find your ball in two of the most awkward of lies: an uphill or a downhill lie.

● ADJUSTMENT FOR THE DOWNHILL LIE ●

1 The loft of a club is decreased from an eight to a seven or six, depending on the steepness of the slope.

2 The ball should be towards the back foot. Your weight is is in front of the ball. From this position it is easier to ensure that you strike the ball first and not hit the ground behind the ball.

3 Restrict body movement by taking only a short backswing, keeping the weight in front of the ball.

4 Don't try for too much length. Ensure that you keep your balance.

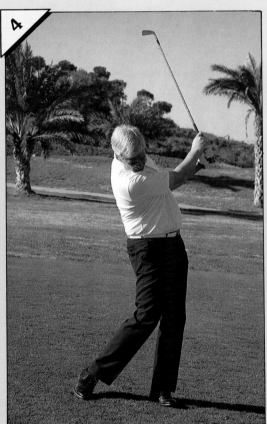

● DOWNHILL ●

You look at the target line with the ground flowing away from you in the downhill lie and you feel that on a flat fairway you might need an 8-iron, say, to pitch the ball onto the green. But you are striking down into the ball because of the slope. Depending on the degree of slope, that position is going to tighten up the loft of the club, giving it the action of a 7-iron or perhaps a 6-iron. It is the same as hooding the club-face over the ball, closing the face, and thus reducing the loft.

Assume a stance where the ball is well back towards the right foot so that you swing directly into it. Take care not to hit the ground first. If you hit the ball first and it goes up and away you will put slice spin on it, like the back spin chopshot in table tennis. The ball will go left and come back to the right. If the lie of the ball allows you to reach for a straighter-faced, less lofted, club, because the target is more than a long pitch away, aim further left. The slice spin should bring it round, if your swing matches your chosen club.

When taking aim, grip the club a little lower than normal – it's called going down the shaft. It will give you more control for this awkward shot. Keep your hands forward of the ball.

You must feel comfortable for this shot, confident that you will not lose your balance as you swing the clubhead through the ball. Flex your knees – the right one will be bent inwards a little to balance your weight on the slope. Begin with a short backswing. Take the club back with your arms, not your shoulders, on a line suggested by the slope of the ground. Keeping your head still will bring confidence that you will not lose your balance as you strike downwards and through the ball.

● ADJUSTMENT FOR THE UPHILL LIE ●

1 The angle of the clubhead is increased. A seven-iron will become an eight- or even a nine-iron, depending on the steepness of the slope.

2 The ball should be in front of the centre line, enabling you to swing through, with the slope, to achieve maximum lift.

The length of the backswing should be determined by the angle of the slope. You must not swing so far back as to lose your balance.

● UPHILL ●

The slope increases the loft of the club so that a 7-iron played on an upward slope will carry the ball the shorter distance of an 8-iron or, on a steeper slope, a 9-iron.

You are swinging into a ball on an uphill slope. This will have the effect of increasing the loft on the club-face. This makes you think twice about club selection. It is not enough to choose a club which will suit the distance. It has to carry enough loft to lift the ball clear of the slope.

Boldness is not your friend when you are facing a ball with your left leg and foot higher than the right. The ball must be struck on the up-swing. This will cause it to have a hook spin, so allow for this built-in movement in the flight by aiming off a little to the right.

Facing a steep slope, you will need height to clear it. You will be tempted towards a stronger club to achieve distance. Do not be too greedy: you may catch the slope and lose distance. Watch out, too, for that natural tendency to move your body weight into the slope on the downswing. This troublemaker means your downswing will lose its arc and will come in too steeply, 'de-lofting' the clubface to lower the trajectory of the ball, which will fly into the slope.

Here is how to play the shot. Stand behind the ball and picture the flight. Seek the target line. Remember the ball will move slightly to the left. Do not be tempted to be too bold. Take aim. Grip the club lower down than normal to give you a little more control. Take your stance with the ball positioned more towards the left foot than the right. Your posture will depend on the steepness of the slope, your left knee bending more than your right, so that your body angle is as near as possible to 90° to the slope. Keep your weight on your right leg so you may sweep through the ball when making the strike. Keep the backswing short to a maximum of a three-quarter swing. Swing through the ball, with a follow–through high enough to ensure that you do not lose your balance.

● ABOVE THE FEET – FLAT SWING ●

1 Take a more upright stance at an angle of 90° to the slope. From this position the swing plane will be flatter than normal.

2 The swing should be within your balance limits. The longer the swing, the greater the likelihood of loss of balance.

3 In the follow-through, keep your head still a little longer than usual.

● ABOVE THE FEET ●

Another tricky situation is playing the ball when it is above your feet, on a slope going upwards from left to right. Balance is always the keystone when building a stance for awkward lies.

Flex your knees so that you have your weight solidly over your feet and can feel that it is not going to slip onto your heels. Once again, go down the shaft a little with your grip to gain more control and allow you to stand closer to the ball. Assume a more than normally upright stance at an angle of 90° to the slope. Take the ball from a spot nearer to the left foot than the right, to help a smooth action through it, when you strike.

The swing must be within your balance limits: the longer the swing, the more likely it is that you will sway away from the ball. The stance will give you a flatter swing plane and, coupled with the fact that the toe of the club will be slightly off the ground, the club-face will close slightly. This gives the ball draw – moving right to left in flight.

Your stance allows you to take a confident swing because there is no restriction on the body turn. With a maximum three-quarter back-swing, concentrate on sweeping the club through the ball to a good high finish.

● BELOW THE FEET – UPRIGHT SWING ●

1 To anchor your balance at the address, your weight should be on your heels. Stick your bottom out more than usual as you flex your knees. From this position the swing plane will be more upright than normal.

2 From this position, the hips will not be able to move, so concentrate on generating power from the shoulder turn.

3 As with shots from all awkward lies, the head should be kept still a little longer than usual to prevent loss of balance.

● BELOW THE FEET ●

When the ball is below the feet, that is on a slope rising from right to left, it presents the most awkward of the four lies discussed here. The amount of slope will determine the distance that you stand from the ball.

To anchor your balance, keep your weight back on your heels as you address the ball. Stick your bottom out a little more than usual as you flex your knees. You can feel immediately that this position will restrict the amount of shoulder and body turn in the swing and will encourage a steeper than normal swing plane.

Your balance is threatened in this shot. You have no shoulder turn to help your swing. You must leave that to your arms and hands. Spread your feet to provide the best chance of balancing confidently.

Aim down to the left of the target. This will help you to keep the clubhead square. Take your stance so that the ball lies in the middle of your feet, and grip the club at the top end of the grip, as you need to use as much of the shaft as you can.

Let your arms and hands control the swing without affecting your balance.

● BUNKER SHOTS ●

Although the word bunker is said to be a Scottish term for receptacle, do not look upon it as being the trash can of your game. While average golfers curse their luck when the little white ball kicks off-line down the fairway and pops into a bunker, most tournament professionals shrug their shoulders. To them, the ball is in a position for an attacking shot.

Bunkers *can* be fearsome, like the infamous 'Hell Bunker' guarding the 14th green on St Andrews Old Course, or 'Hell's Half-acre' the biggest bunker in the world, at the 7th at Pine Valley, New Jersey; or they can be shallow traps laid well down the fairway to catch the wayward tiger-line drivers. Not only are they all shapes and sizes, but the sand within them sometimes differs even around the same course.

To discover what you have to beat, you need to be in the bunker getting the feel through your feet. But before you ever go into a sand bunker at all, there are two rules that you must always remember. The first is that you may only ground the club in striking the shot. If you touch the sand while in the address position or in the course of the backswing you will be penalized. When addressing the ball therefore, make sure that your clubhead is clear of the sand. It is better to hold it three inches (75 mm) above the ball at the address position than ¹⁄₁₆ inch (1.5 mm) too low.

The second thing to remember is that when you have played your shot out of the bunker, always rake the sand flat, both where you have played the shot and where you have made foot marks walking in to play the shot. However, this carries no penalty, unless a golf club committee has made a local rule.

One other thing worth mentioning is that when you are taking your stance in a bunker to address the ball, you are allowed to twist your feet into the sand. This will give you a good solid base from which to start your swing, and it will give you an idea of the depth and texture of the sand in the bunker.

The club for bunker play is, not unnaturally, the sand wedge, which is designed with three outstanding features: it is the heaviest club, which helps when striking down and into the sand; it has the greatest loft of all golf clubs to help lift the sand and ball up and away; and it has a flange which will level off the clubhead as it travels under the ball.

● BUNKER SHOT STANCE ●

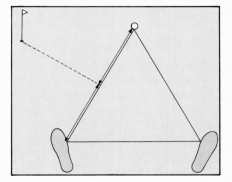

For the standard bunker shot, visualize a line from the flag bisecting the triangle of feet and ball.

TOP AND ABOVE Imagine there is a circle around the ball which is the white of a fried egg; the ball itself is the yolk. When taking the shot, strike the sand behind the ball, sending the sand and the ball onto the green.

LEFT When addressing the ball for a sand shot, make sure the club is well clear of the sand.

LEFT It is a penalty for the clubhead to touch the sand, except when it actually strikes at the ball.

LEFT You are allowed to twist your feet into the sand to give you a solid base from which to start your swing. It also gives you an idea of the depth and texture of the sand.

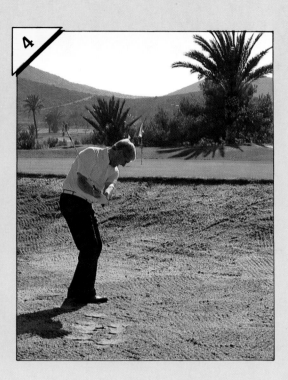

● THE SHORT BUNKER SHOT ●

1 Remember that a trap shot can be an attacking shot.

2 Even in a bunker, stand behind the ball and always look for the target line.

3 Always point to the left of the target with both feet and shoulders.

4 The wrist must break early in the swing.

5 The length of backswing will be determined by the length of the shot.

6 Strike the sand behind the ball.

7 Make sure you follow through to control the flight of the ball.

● THE SUNNY-SIDE UP SHOT ●

When you see your ball roll or pitch into a sand trap, do not let your hopes fade. For you could be facing a 'sunny-side up' shot. Look at the ball lying in the bunker and imagine it is a fried egg lying there sunny-side up. The ball is the yolk and the sand circle around it the white. Take your sand wedge and note the big flange on it. You have to use this to take that fried egg out of the sand, white and yolk together.

Line up your feet and your shoulders, pointing slightly left of the target – an out-to-in plane. When you come through the shot, as you must, the flanged clubhead will cut nicely under the fried egg, exploding it onto the green. The strength of the shot and the amount of sand you take will determine its length.

● THE EXPLOSION SHOT ●

To explode out of the sand, lay your clubhead open with the bottom of the blade square to the target. This will force your hands to be forward of the ball. Aim your feet left of the target and open to the target line, with your shoulders pointing in the same direction. Shuffle your feet into the sand. This will put them slightly below the ball and help you in taking some sand with the shot. This stance should allow the ball to be well forward. Take the hands down the club grip just a little. The swing should be long and slow, rather than a short, quick swing. Swing the club back smoothly, breaking the wrists almost straight away to the top of the backswing. Then bring the clubhead down and across the line striking the sand two inches (50 mm) behind the ball to send the sand and the ball onto the green. *The clubhead does not hit the ball.* It is the force of it striking down into the sand behind the ball which propels the ball upward onto the green.

TOP RIGHT When playing up the slope from a bunker you cannot use the sunny-side up shot without adjustment, because there is no cushion of sand behind the ball. Try to compensate for this by leaning with the slope as far as possible so that, in effect, you are playing from flat sand.

TOP FAR RIGHT You are permitted to settle your feet into the sand; this will give you a firmer base and some feel for the sand's consistency.

RIGHT When the ball is plugged, take up a square stance and hit through the sand with the clubhead square to the ball.

FAR RIGHT If you are in a fairway bunker and therefore want to gain distance with the shot, it is better to stand on the surface of the sand to avoid giving the ball excessive loft.

● THE LONG BUNKER SHOT ●

Bunkers are placed as hazards around the course, not only to guard the green, but to make approach shots more challenging. You will need to know how to play the long shot out of one of these bunkers, where the object is to get the greatest distance.

The club you need must be able to achieve the maximum distance but must also be able to lift the ball clear of the bunker wall. Long bunkers, sometimes laid to trap the long hitter, have low walls so you may be safe playing a mid iron or even a longer iron. Do not gamble by taking a club which has to be perfectly struck to be safe. Play the percentage game. Remember that with this shot, if you hit the sand before the ball, you will lose many yards. Think of a clean hit.

In taking up your stance do not shuffle the feet deep into the sand to make a deep base. This will set you too low and lessen your chance of clearing the lip of the bunker cleanly. Just twist the soles of your shoes into the sand to get a firm base from which to swing. Take a stance so that the ball is positioned towards the front foot, your knees bent only slightly to keep the swing above the ground. Look at the top of the ball rather than behind it. This will further help you to achieve a clean hit. Employ a full follow-through.

● GAINING DISTANCE FROM THE BUNKER ●

1 The disciplines involved in this shot are no different from any other shot you play. Stand behind the ball looking towards the target. Find the target line.

2 Address the ball, making sure that the clubhead does not touch the sand.

3 and **4** Stand more upright than usual, looking at the top of the ball.

5 and **6** Don't over-swing, as this will cause a swaying movement.

7 For the long sand shot, a high follow-through will help ensure a good, clean hit and achieve maximum distance.

ABOVE The rough at La Manga golf club is not severe; courses in a dry climate do not have the long summer grass found off many European fairways.

OPPOSITE If you are unlucky enough to land in a divot, use a club with more loft and take up a stance with the ball well back toward the inside of the right shoe. This will help you to achieve a more effective chopping action, driving the clubhead down and through the ball.

● FROM THE ROUGH ●

When you find yourself in the rough, the only plan you should have in your mind is to get out. Be satisfied to find a line which will get you back on the fairway. Do not be too ambitious.

Your normal, smooth, free swing can spell danger. The clubhead arc will shave the ground at the start of the backswing, at the bottom of the downswing and at the beginning of the follow-through. If the rough is thick, it will tangle the clubhead causing problems with the shot. You must visualize an action which will strike into the back of the ball, without getting the clubhead caught up in the grass. You must strike down into the ball on a steeper arc than normal. Select a lofted club. This will help to get more flight.

If the rough is slight, take the ball in the middle of a slightly open stance. The thicker the rough gets, the further back from the ball your stance should be.

Grip the club down the shaft a little for more control, but do not attempt a full swing. A three-quarter swing will be sufficient – even a half swing might be best for the job. And don't worry about the follow-through – just let it happen. Indeed sometimes you might not be able to follow through at all because of the lie.

The important thing is to concentrate on bringing the clubhead into the ball at an angle. The angle will be determined by the lie and the thickness of the grass around the ball.

● ESCAPING FROM THE ROUGH ●

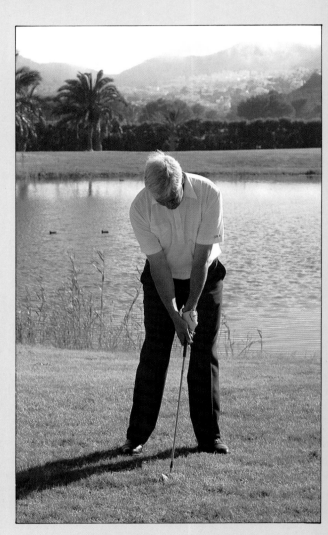

3 Stand with your weight slightly in front of the ball, enabling you to strike downward, which ensures that the ball is struck before the ground.

1 (INSET) Line up the shot, looking for the all-important target line.

2 When addressing the ball, make sure you do not press your club down behind the ball as this could improve the lie and thus incur penalty shots.

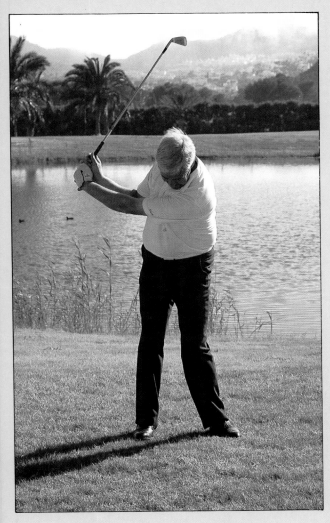

4 Take a backswing which will not unbalance you.

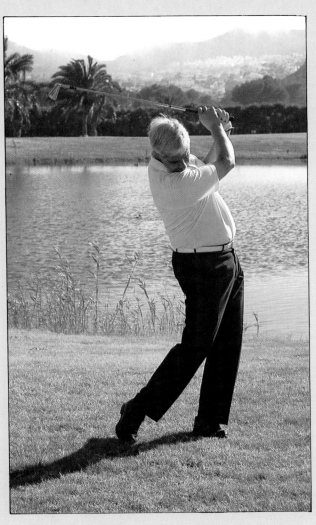

5 Strike through the ball, keeping your head still to ensure a solid contact.

● LOW SHOT – STRONGER CLUB ●

1 You will often be faced with hitting a low shot, either under the wind or under some trees.

2 Look towards the pin, find the target line.

3 Select a club to achieve the required distance without using your full swing. The harder you hit the ball the higher it will fly. A stronger club than necessary, with an easier swing, will result in a lower trajectory.

4 Do not unbend at the waist as you go through the ball and don't follow through too far.

● LOW SHOTS ●

Many times in your rounds of golf you will want to play a low shot. Perhaps overhanging branches of a tree are impeding your path to the green.

Remember that the harder you hit the ball, the higher it will fly. With this in mind, when you have pictured the shot and worked out your club selection, take at least one club stronger, or better still two clubs stronger, than you need. The more club you have to spare, the easier your swing can be, while still achieving the required distance. You will therefore keep the ball lower.

You will need to keep your weight slightly in front of the ball throughout the shot. Gripping down the club will help to give you a shorter, more compact swing. The tendency when playing from this forward position is to close the club-face, so aim a little to the right of target. Position yourself further back from the ball in your stance than you normally would for the club selected. Then swing nice and slow, keeping the swing short and easy, not letting your weight move behind the ball.

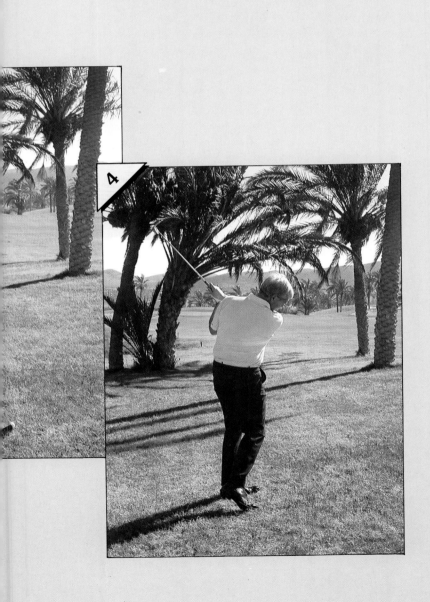

● HIGH SHOTS ●

If you can play high shots confidently, you can make nonsense of the planned hazards of bunkers and the natural hazards of trees which suddenly get in your way. You soar over them.

The rough guide lines for this shot are naturally the opposite of those for the low shot. The harder you hit the ball, the higher it flies. You throttled back the fullness of your swing for the low shot, now you open it up again for the high shot. The swing is full and firm, and the club is one which is going to make the ball clear the hazard. Fix it into your mind that you are going to do just that: clear the hazard.

Stand behind the ball and line up where you intend to fly and land the ball. Forget eating up extra distance. You are seeking take-off, flight and happy landings in this short-haul shot. With the shot picture in your mind select the club with sufficient loft for the planned flight. Take aim. Position the ball nearer to your front foot than you normally would with that particular club. When making your swing, make sure that the full loft of the club is square to the ball and your body weight, although moving onto your left foot, stays behind the ball.

The common error in making this shot is over-enthusiasm. Too much strength is put into the swing in an attempt to smash the ball out and over trouble, causing the body to lunge forward. This sway de-lofts the club, cancels out the specially designed asset, the angle of its club-face, and causes loss of height, resulting in too early a touchdown.

● AVOIDING TROUBLE WITH THE HIGH SHOT ●

1 You will need to hit the ball high on occasion, to clear trees or overhanging branches.

2 When standing behind the ball and looking for the target line, think height! Select a club to clear the trees easily and don't gamble.

3 Address the ball in a forward stance, keeping your weight behind the ball.

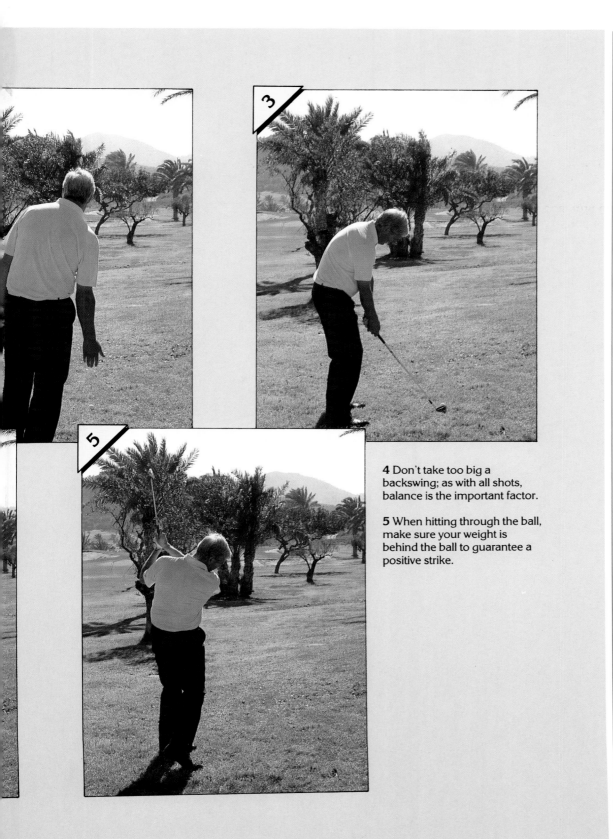

4 Don't take too big a backswing; as with all shots, balance is the important factor.

5 When hitting through the ball, make sure your weight is behind the ball to guarantee a positive strike.